STORAGE ISSUES

THE DREAMSEEKER POETRY SERIES

Books in the DreamSeeker Poetry Series, intended to make available fine writing by Anabaptist-related poets, are published by Cascadia Publishing House under the DreamSeeker Books imprint and often copublished with Herald Press. Cascadia oversees content of these poetry collections in collaboration with the DreamSeeker Poetry Series Editor Jeff Gundy (Jean Janzen volumes 1-4) as well as in consultation with its Editorial Council and the authors themselves.

1. On the Cross
   By Dallas Wiebe, 2005
2. I SAW GOD DANCING
   By Cheryl Denise Miller, 2005
3. Evening Chore
   By Shari Wagner, 2005
4. Where We Start
   By Debra Gingerich, 2007
5. The Coat Is Thin
   By Leonard Neufeldt
6. Miracle Temple
   By Esther Stenson
7. Storage Issues
   By Suzanne Miller
8. Face to Face
   By Julie Cadwallader-Staub

   Also worth noting are two poetry collections that would likely have been included in the series had it been in existence then:
1. Empty Room with Light
   By Ann Hostetler, 2002

2. A Liturgy for Stones
   By David Wright, 2003

STORAGE ISSUES

Poems 1988-2008

SUZANNE KAY MILLER

DreamSeeker Poetry Series, Volume 7

DreamSeeker Books
TELFORD, PENNSYLVANIA

an imprint of
Cascadia Publishing House LLC

Cascadia Publishing House orders, information, reprint permissions:
contact@CascadiaPublishingHouse.com
1-215-723-9125
126 Klingerman Road, Telford PA 18969
www.CascadiaPublishingHouse.com

Storage Issues
Copyright © 2010 by Suzanne Kay Miller
All rights reserved
DreamSeeker Books is an imprint of Cascadia Publishing House LLC
Library of Congress Catalog Number: 2010004460
ISBN 13: 978-1-931038-76-8; ISBN 10: 1-931038-76-7
Book design by Cascadia Publishing House
Cover design by Gwen M. Stamm

The paper used in this publication is recycled and meets the minimum requirements of American National Standard for Information Sciences—Permanence of Paper for Printed Library Materials, ANSI Z39.48-1984.1984

Versions of poems in this collection have appeared in various outlets. For a complete listing, see Credits section, back of book.

Library of Congress Cataloguing-in-Publication Data
Miller, Suzanne Kay.
  Storage issues : poems, 1988-2008 / Suzanne Kay Miller.
    p. cm. -- (Dreamseeker poetry series ; v. 7)
  Includes bibliographical references.
  Summary: "Storage Issues pictures an individual wandering through the remains of communal life. These personal lyric and narrative poems search for meaning in the background, events, and concerns of one Mennonite woman's existence." "[summary]"--Provided by publisher.
  ISBN-13: 978-1-931038-76-8 (trade pbk. : alk. paper)
  ISBN-10: 1-931038-76-7 (trade pbk. : alk. paper)
  I. Title.
  PS3613.I557S76 2010
  811'.6--dc22
                              2010004460

15 14 13 12 11 10   10 9 8 7 6 5 4 3 2 1

*To Susan Kay Unruh Reitz and
William James Buchhorn*

TABLE OF CONTENTS

3 A.M. • 15
A Billion Times Told • 16
After the Flood • 18
Awake Before the Baby Cries • 19
Balloons • 20
Born Again • 21
Breaking Bud • 22
Carriages • 23
Cat in the Christmas Tree • 25
Come Close • 27
Condensation • 28
Conservative Bodies • 30
Dreamers • 31
Feminine • 32
Finding Anna • 33
Formal Failure • 35
Formless • 36
Forty-Six • 37
Four Sticks • 38
Girls Playing Church • 41
Grandma • 42
Gruff as Necessary • 43
Highway • 44
How Can We Know? • 45
How Much More • 47

Hulda, You Are Leaving • 49
Hulda, You Left Word • 50
I Know, Carol, You Are Dying • 51
In the City at Twenty • 52
It Was the Kind • 54
Knowledge of Birds • 55
Leaves on the River • 56
Leaving Wichita Late • 57
Living under Authority • 58
Loose Woman • 60
Moved by Emptiness • 61
Mrs. Jacob Buller's Grave • 62
Mrs. Jacob Buller's Wedding • 63
Old Story • 64
On Entering Grandma's House • 67
Outside • 68
Photographs • 69
Prodigal • 71
Psalm 1 • 72
Rearranging Furniture • 73
Red-Tailed Hawks • 75
Remember • 76
Riddles from Mary • 77
Round House • 78
Scissors • 79
Shingles, Socks, and Photographs • 80
Silence • 81
Storage Issues • 82

String Bag • 83
Sunday Evening • 84
The Matchbox • 85
The Old Land • 86
The Revenger's Tragedy • 89
Thy Waves • 90
To My Daughter Jailed in Chicago: 3/20/03 • 91
Try This • 92
Vachel Lindsay's Piano Moon • 93
Vision • 94
We Place These Stones • 95
We Wait for Words • 97
Wedding Rings • 98
Wheat • 99
Winter Light • 101
Witness • 102
Women's Work • 103
Yggdrasill • 104

Credits   105
The Author   107

Alphabet works better
than time because it is

both tangible and creative
with raw material without

requiring conscientious
people to read into, much

less understand, a plan.
A search for meaning strays

beyond meaning since alphabets
are arbitrary. If contents

are to be creative, they must
be new patterns in timeless soup.

STORAGE ISSUES

3 A.M.

She wakes a moment
before roots tear rock.

She weeps as nails
shred canopy.

She jerks in bed
when shoulder hits carpet.

She hears the tree fall
when it falls alone.

A Billion Times Told
"The Windhover" —Gerard Manley Hopkins

She wept profusely for an hour,
which did nothing to comfort her mother,
who had decided, though it seemed early,
to prepare her for womanhood because
she had been swinging so widely of late.
They sat on the couch, alone in the house.

The mother had driven her home
since she had refused again to enter
the Sunday School. They'd have to
go back at noon to pick up the father
and the other children. It's a holy thing
when a married couple loves each other,

her mother said in a sad, sweet voice
moved by pity and fear. She kept up
her wash of tears like a thunderstorm
she could watch through a window.
Four years since her sister's birth
and her question: If the baby comes

from the mother, why do people
say it looks like its father? She remembered
her mother, ironing, promising the answer
on a day when she could understand.
Maybe crying was the dam of all her
ignorance finally overflowed, maybe breached.

For years, she wondered if a woman would have to
take off her underpants for the miracle to occur.
She felt stupid for not knowing. Tables turned
when she came home ruined at nineteen,
and her mother cried that she didn't understand
how you could do it with someone you didn't love.

She quickly married a man who resembled the children
she wanted. And, after another nineteen years,
her husband begged her mother to help him
reach his wife. When she saw her mother at her door,
she ran to lock herself in her bedroom. But her mother
ran, too, and got her foot in the door.

She leaned hard to keep it closed, but there was crying
on the other side—more than for a foot—so she let
her in; they locked the door and cried together.
The mother said, We knew it was bad, but we didn't
want to say anything; we thought
that would make it worse.

She had to fall apart to shine—consider blue-bleak
embers, ah my dear. But she knows that fall, gall
and gash burn down. She is considering dropping
from some great height into the steady air.
She can't wait for another to answer her questions.
Buckle! She needs some mastery of the thing.

After the Flood

Like Noah, I started drinking after the flood.
One learns to cultivate a life apart
from responsibility. To live as an island
in a sea of wickedness, even with God,
leaves one dry. In the sorrow
that knows comfort in resignation,
I sometimes drink alone. What you do
is up to you. If you should see me lying naked
and refuse to laugh, by God you are blessed.

Awake Before the Baby Cries

Twenty minutes before sunrise
deep red of low eastern clouds
veined with blowing black branches
is her sore throat wide on a slideshow.

Silhouettes of cedars pray,
nod, bow to the north,
stretch forth long-fingered hands
from long-sleeved robes.

In orange air, I wish I would
have papaya juice for her.
The sun appears—a honey-lemon-
menthol-eucalyptus lozenge

in green and yellow clouds.

Balloons

pushed by wriggling string tails to heaven's womb,
watched as tenderly as the sparrows and as those few
entangled in bony branches and hairy evergreen arms—
Easter morning, the congregation letting go, and yet,
it's Resurrection, not Ascension, Day, shouldn't we

be watching our dead for signs? Be wrestling Browning
Cleon?—*Freed by the throbbing impulse we call death,*
We burst there as the worm into the fly,
Who while a worm still, wants his wings. But no!
But yes! We must imagine what is *not yet revealed*,

what may arise from hope's annihilation. We don't,
after all, remember the ecstasy of our conception. What
about doves? the gentler-minded have asked. What
good bright, burst balloons? Why not chickens which
lead to eggs—the brunch, the hunt, the jelly beans?

Balloons resemble flying jelly beans. Remember that
impulse to stretch and slip out into the open world—
does death strain like birth in both fear and pleasure?

I wouldn't mean to make light of death in branches.
The line between bawdiness, holiness, and terror
is fine; in death, maybe finer. We sing our fragile air.

Born Again
for Abe

He calls me as he walks from his car
past shingled houses fenced in driftwood
to the beach over low tide sand—the farthest
wave of his leaving—and then holds the phone

farther—the stretch of his arm over water,
so I can hear the ocean, the wind,
the birds, breathe salt again, gaze west
over my dining room table in Kansas

and feel those waters break.

Breaking Bud

Bless God, bless God
for a slim striped dirt-colored frog
in the first flush of deadnettle, milkweed
and bindweed unmaking the hollyhock bed.

Bless God, bless God
for the first mourning dove,
a scissortail flycatcher calm on the fence
and a cardinal crazy with the pulse of a branch in his grasp.

Bless God, bless God
for blades and sprays
or runner-rooted grass homesteading the edge
of the warming crushed-fossil laden road.

Bless God, bless God
for an old exposed nest
luring me near to touch unfolded leaves
in the last local species of trees to break bud.

Carriages

The first ended with the death of the child,
the first to hear her heart, three days before
the wedding.

Then one night of stars circumscribing her body,
her second child ended her first worldview. Alone
on the apartment patio, she looked up and bled.
Her daughter emerged after sunrise, taught her
images and instincts of her second worldview.
She babbled, lost the language of the overgrown
city, tripped in the rubble beneath her feet.

When she carried her third child, she ground teeth
in her sleep, swished whisky for pain, craved thick
black bean soup. When he unwound, straightened,
and shot out with the sinewy strength of a jackrabbit
hurtling toward the moon half an hour before midnight,
he refused first breath while he looked around blue.
Then he used his lungs but refused further comfort.

Carrying her fourth, she shoveled her husband's soil,
cursed her pain, hung out wet laundry and cooked
the breakfast before she rounded a bend and met
a canoe-tipping boulder that threw her into their
unmade bed. He met land in his father's rough hands,
screamed to ensure attention, fed and slept while the
midwife tied things up, soothed the stirred-up stream.

"I dreamed a woman came in too far along to make it
to the hospital and gave birth on this table," the strip-mall
doctor joked as she flung the placenta into the plastic bowl,
which she forgot in the drama of the ambulance transfer,
had to retrieve later. Hearing his sleep-breathing at home
that night, she knew her fourth child would be easy to forget
in dramatic scenes, would always be accompanied by
    dreams.

The last again ended in its early death.
Lying down for an hour, she looked up
to children watching closely.

Cat in the Christmas Tree
—Dante, *Paradiso*, IX. 7-9

I think the cat is Jesus when I rock
crocheting, watching *Home Alone* and he
creeps onto my lap and bumps his head

against my chin and leans into my heart,
the way I think a man is God when he
talks soft and lets me lean on him. I know

many cats will live in homes without
other cats. Do their mamas purr
a visceral imprint deep into their guts

in those long days their eyes are pasted shut?
Abandonment will take its toll. This cat cries
out his night each morning while I wake.

Meows grate. I trip on twining. He jumps
on and off my lap with less whining,
more purring. When purring steadies him

in happiness, he climbs the Christmas tree.
He knocks a few fake branches from the trunk
far beneath the holy star. His orange eyes

hold steady, round and calm behind the blinking
string of lights and colored wooden beads.
I close my eyes to seek sufficiency

I carry deep from someone. A vision would help,
a voice, something to drink, a living touch—
Goodness, what suffices would be enough.

Come Close

You, come close, whispers the tree the sky
parted from ground with all its gathered strength.
Stop your car. Don't be afraid you'll cry
among the ruined leaves. Walk the length
of broken trees. And though the wreckage shocks,
awful it is not. Though wrapped in strips
of ragged tin and single muddy socks,
surviving branches still hear coyote yips
on misty nights. Why do you stay away
from broken trees? Is it the mix of dry
with green? Empathize. You know decay
and brokenness within your life. Don't lie.
Confess to pain. Endure with mouse and deer.
Come close, and you won't turn away from here.

Condensation

The nightmare about being found out:
hiding under the window in the corner

with a man who does not know
it was she who tipped off the police;

she counts every motion of his turning
until betrayal dawns.

Even when safe, lying at night
with a good man, nightmares

leave her unable to move:
In one, she had started

to eat from a holiday table, no more
than a carrot, when they told her

that was not allowed;
in another, she combed her hair

in a new style which set off
allergic reactions

in those she did not
want to hurt. She will

always be afraid
of betraying her betrayers.

Threats linger as in the kind
of fog she sees

in winter driving home:
the road ahead,

the stars beyond,
but a veil at eye-level,

a rising river of warm, moist air
discovered by the bearing-down cold.

Conservative Bodies

Take an idea and allow its trajectory
to continue undeflected for five hundred years
and its position may be quite distant
from the unity of its origins

is what I would say to you now
that you are dead and I have had time
to create a defense, which has not been easy
given my training in defenselessness.

You scared me when you raised your skirt higher
than the bottom of your girdle with its garters
to show me how you would look if you wore
an outfit like the one my mother

dressed me in. I said nothing then,
but started reading theology too soon
and worked to make my dresses longer
than my mother's wishes. How far

out have I spun? Were you frantic to save me
from my legs, or screaming that I should run?

Dreamers

While we slept, it snowed.
With curtains drawn around us,
warm within the darkness,
we lay still for hours.
Outside snow grew deep.

We dreamed of what we knew,
but while we slept, it snowed.
The world we knew lay changed.
The world we knew grew white
since last it had been light.

Light through frozen panes
melts our sleeping stillness.
While we slept, it snowed!
Waking tells of change
happening outside us.

Waking tells of change.
New dreams in us flow—
daydreams bright and frozen,
for while we slept, it snowed.
Night dreams do not keep.

Night dreams do not keep,
for what they tell is past.
Strong dreams make the present.
This day grows old fast.
Then while we sleep, it snows.

Feminine

Grounded in my knowledge of blood
born gravel flowing over and through
me, grounded in my knowledge

of unnamed waiting poised
in my own measured gaze, I know
the feminine broods in the void

and in her wish for form
before sensing shade or fragrance.
She lifts me out of water
and lays me on the ground.

She lights a candle, and I
smell smoke, see flame, press wax,
hear wind, breathe her breath, sense her waiting
past the edge of light brooding.

Finding Anna

When I cannot find you lying five west
and eleven south of your husband,
my great grandfather, or one west
and six north of your daughter,
my grandmother, I drive four miles east,

slip through a barbed wire fence
and an ancient rise of grass. Crying,
lewd, stern, and angry voices
lose themselves in the hush.
I can step off the prairie,

follow a cow path down the washout,
and find you in the creek, shoulder
deep, your white hair and white gown
rippling across your body barely
weighted in the current,

remove my shoes,
shirt and jeans, and slip into my white
robe to lie with you beneath the willow.
The sand and water are cool.
Your eyes are pools.

Minnows between our toes!
Left to ourselves, the air
empty of intrusion, the pasture
still above and beside us,
we may grow into moss—

long strands anchored to calico
pebbles, food and shelter
for fish, delicacy for deer.
Moss or women,
we have loved this place.

Formal Failure

How perfectly the rooftop frost remains
in chimney, dormer and dark cedar shapes.
The morning sun is always gone by noon.
These shadows like the moon live sacrifice—
only embrace at arm's length for the sake
of form. Compare this with the lectionary
changing in a slow and ordinary
way through sorrow's day and night without
release to spin in premature delight.
The formal failure of the distance in
the universe will hold until it breaks
into consummation. Meanwhile, the moon
dances for the earth, and the sun defines
restraint, matches shadow with every face.

Formless

Proverbs bang
on my bedroom door.
I am sleeping in!
Where is harm
in sleeping late?
I accept the rest!
I know much
does not depend
on consciousness.

In the antiverbal
sense, formless,
in it deep,
without a light,
I shall wait
for that mighty
invisible wind
to create
a floor and feet.

Forty-Six

I finally see the ruts
at forty-six—a day trip
to points along the Santa Fe Trail—
five miles west of Council Grove,
seven-tenths east, a twenty foot swale.
Thousands of pounds of cargo
in thousands of wagons
pulled by thousands of oxen
and mules wear the ground
down—a hundred and fifty
years do not raise it.

We talk about where we are,
how we got here, where
we're going now that child
support is ending, and alimony
is gone; the good men are
busy; the bad aren't sorry, and
our jobs don't support us.
We're trying to keep this simple.
The years don't raise
what's been ground down,
but on either side
the scenery is lovely,
and many have already made it.

Four Sticks

I, Karolina, learned how to play
from my mother, Wilhelmina.

My earliest memories
are of days such as these:
going to sleep under stars,
tucked in close to Mama's side,
hearing her whisper, "See,

there is the milk the children spilled.
It runs across the sky.
And look at all the crumbs
fallen from the table.
Those children must be full now,
tucked into soft beds,
rocked to sleep by breezes.
They will dream of heaven
all night long."

Before I awoke, in those days,
Papa picked me up
and laid me in a little bed
fixed in the top of the handcart.
I would wake to a bumping ride,
see a bright, clean-swept sky,
and find a piece of bread
tucked in a fold beside me.

I would run with the children
most of the walking-day,
but when we stopped
in the hot afternoon,
Mama taught me how to play.

"Come, Karolina; find four sticks.
These will be the corners.
Find two more for a door.
Wrap this twine from one to the next.
See how the door can open?
Bring your dolly from the cart.
I will get a pan. We can make
a pie with mud. Sprinkle
ashes across the top.
This little branch can be your broom.
What a fine house you have!"

"Do we live in heaven now?"
I asked Mama that winter
in the large house, warm
and full of lights, where we lodged
until spring when Papa
could build a house of our own.

Forty years later, we left
Russia, my home, my mother—
Johann and I, our seven children—
the future drawing us farther.

If I had not learned to play,
what would I have done
when Anna and Elizabeth cried
in the days without a home?

If I had not seen that children
live so well among the stars,
how could I have walked away
from the graves of Maria, Helena,
Cornelius and Peter?

Girls Playing Church

The stairs, perfect as pews, begin
at the dining room, lead to the bedrooms.
Does Ken really belong to Barbie?
He never more than stiffly kisses her. If they are,

in fact, soft, they hide themselves like turtles.
Their clothes stretch better than their bodies.
Though we know bodies are worth more
than clothes, Barbie and Ken remind us

of our parents in their Sunday clothes.
Our baby dolls flop through the rituals—
Cheerios, silent threats, cradles created from hand-
kerchiefs, hushes, small tablets, finger play.

We let Barbie and Ken be older children
who can sit still. The oldest among us stands up
for a short sermon—long sitting straight wearies
mothers with children. Others take turns

leading singing: announcing verses one,
two and five; lifting arms in the graceful
upbeat; singing a first note out
on the down. Some of the babies see

the dust motes rising in the light falling
from the window at the top of the stairs
we would need to twist ourselves to see.

Grandma

She said, Let this be your last child.
    It will be too much for you.

  I said, I think my life has been normal,
    but I have not known how to speak
    of pain as you did.

She said, Get yourself a pretty dress.

  I said, I don't know how.
    It is very complicated.

She said, You must ask and hint.
    Mostly, you have to want it.

  I said, I have worked hard not to want
    the same things you wanted.

She said, As your face grows older,
    you will see it is all the same—
    a new dress, the need for love;
    new dishes, hope.

  I said, Here. I made you coffee.

She said, Yes, and sugar
    makes it good.

Gruff as Necessary

I lock my bedroom door now,
keep a working smoke alarm,
put my box springs on the floor—
no room for monsters any more.

I am the last to check the locks,
alarms and lights and invoke strength—
I walk the night-bridge last.

My little goats know what to say
as split hooves drop as tiny rain
stirring upon a spring-fed burn:
*We're sure you want the biggest one
who crosses after us.*

And my almost-grown goats know,
banging boards like a loose screen door
on this windy April night,
I will fix the latch; they, too,
hold the key to cross.

I follow like a snapping sheet
on a Kansas clothesline and no troll
with any sense will dare
a tangle with this mother.

Highway

Melted sky quivers up the road
like a quiet, running creek.

When elusive pools no longer run
I shall stop this car,

lose my shoes, cool my toes, swim,
maybe fly, in blue shallows of the sky.

How Can We Know?
"Among School Children" —W. B. Yeats

She would not
have done that

if she had
known, as in

horror films
where the lead

heads into
monster slime.

"Don't go!" but
in she goes.

And like she,
we cannot

know ourselves
from our scripts

or, O Yeats,
from our art

or our youth.
We can know

poems that do
not know squat

in shadows
in drafty rooms.

How Much More

*If then God so clothe the grass, which is to day in the field,
    and to morrow is cast into the oven; how much more you,
    O ye of little faith?* —Luke 12:28 (KJV)

Accusing Anabaptists, 1552,
Gellius Faber, a Lutheran,
said their rules had "driven some
to despair, and some to suicide."
Menno Simons answered, 1554,
"I have always taught
that all sins...repented of
are pardoned in the blood...."

Warm, addictive, the bright flame falls.
The unsustainable coal is smoke:
resolve finally, perhaps to rise—
light, a fragrant offering.

One drives his car into a semi stopped at a light.
A girl asks her mother gardening,
"Isn't that terrible?"
Mother answers from the soil,
"You don't know what you don't know."

So someone somewhere will not know
what to do with secrets left,
pressed flowers. He took
only one, death.
Shall we burn or scatter petals?
Christ rose, at least, to explain.

Life in Eden is one thing,
in dust and sorrow another. Why
did God sew for them? Why
in the face of unmanageable knowledge
encourage farming? And babies?
Why were Eve and her Adam not,
as promised, killed outright?

What do we do with rules
always learned and taught?
Why are we still living here?
Some are driven to despair.
Flowers dry like blood.
Is the accusation clear?
Why do you kill and sew for us,
reflected image, counting hair?

Hulda, You Are Leaving

Veins in your hands dry like flowers'
stems. Veins in your hands repeat
scenes from ten thousand feet—
turquoise rivers, charcoal highways,

seams in a crazy quilt map. A scene
your hand signs begins in your childhood.
Farther back, I waited in you,
rock in whom I have lain unseen.

I hold your cold hand, mine crosshatched
as a rusty screen, yours transparent
as an infant's face. Your skin is fallen
petals. Your head is light as dried flowers.

Your feet, though covered, are cold.
You are drawing warmth in as you leave.

Hulda, You Left Word

I found you dead.
The black bird spread
from its springing cedar,
spiraled to its telephone wire:
"Like this!"

Two migrating
yellow-headed blackbirds
held still
in the old maize stubble.

A sparrow sat near the road
as I drove by. That same bird
still sat in the same spot
as I drove back by—
first time, looked at me;
second time, looked away.

I nearly hit the mourning doves
on the last stretch of gravel road home.
They rose like snuffed wicks smoke.

I Know, Carol, You Are Dying

I hurt you if I touch you.
Newborn lilac leaves tremble.
All creation groans.

Darkness comes quickly and soon.
Dust sops up the afternoon.
Chicken yards and fields

enter through window sills.
You wait like a drought-
starved animal lying

on open ground rasping
"buzzards," whispering "rocks."
Elm trees shuffle ashamed.

In the City at Twenty

In the leaves of November, she walks
by cold-skinned brick and stone
and windows offering shoes,
pies, groceries, books.

In the bank, she counts her quarters
through the smaller than hand-sized opening
to the teller who knows her number.

She continues up the hill to the light-green stucco,
through two glass doors, one needs a key,
up two twists of stairs and down the dim hallway.

She has met many men who know what they want.
In April, she finds herself staying in
for three raining days. She thinks the streets
are flooded. She does not rise

when her boyfriend buzzes,
the restaurant calls, and her mother calls.
She turns on the radio and hears

a long piece called "Flight of the Snow Geese."
She drops her boyfriend and starts
looking for a different job. Of course,

she has to live through the night his friends
all beg through his locked door for an answer
from his kitchen where he has laid his head
in an apartment-sized gas oven.

It Was the Kind

for Leia

It was the kind of wedding where
the grandmother, judging the moment
undecreed, would query, "So,
when did they get married?"
Was it when they read
the Berry poem; when they slid
their homemade rings; when we sang
a hymn to nature; when
the preacher's, groom's, and bride's words spun;
when *Danaus plexippus* glid
the grassy aisle through us and through
the light between their faces; when
they touched; when in the past
pairings began or in the present they divine
and we can only wonder?

Knowledge of Birds

The raven comes to him who fears the pain
of separation will be more to bear
than can be born, to her who plays despair
upon a silent screen. Some birds retain
the air of truth, so, matching silent saneness
with a body that can fly, I dare
to grope for messages within their stare.
I ease the terror empty air and chain
associations bring when touch is gone.
Dear ones of mine who left without farewell,
sometimes I think you pity me below
and send a word. But, maybe, on their own,
birds see me looking up for clues and tell
themselves, "By grace, if we stare back, she'll know."

Leaves on the River

Leaves line up in the wind
on the river as do geese—
facing into it, falling behind
the leaf or goose before.

When first geese studied leaves
on water, they started to draw
diagrams, honk quiet theories
of wave and flight: the wind

is, thus, one with the river;
moved, draws motion. As wings
beat, leaves appear to know,
are known, and carried so.

Leaving Wichita Late

I drive out of the street and into the highway—
a star, true west. It's been so long,
I say star

instead of planet, instead of Venus.

The eyes of a deer
appear behind my eyes, and I pray
that she turn now,
that we not meet—

highway is road and field in this dark fall—

for her sake, not mine.
Why should she suffer?
But also for mine

since prayer requires this distance.

Living under Authority

Chinese astronomers Hi and Ho were put to death
for failing to foretell the solar eclipse of 2169 BC.
I myself was taken by surprise in 1979. A sifting
of light pulled me away from my baby's morning

nap and onto the edge of the porch. A line
in the west, a leading edge of shadow
dividing light and darkness, swept toward me,
then over me. I was in darkness. Silent stars

stepped forward. The hubbub of birds held still
for a moment of minutes. Then from the west,
again, fast-forward dawn, a broom
shaking birds and brushing out stars.

Fifteen years later, my children ready
for the school bus say an almost total eclipse
will come today. (Oh, Hi and Ho, had you not
children in school?) I turn on the television,

expecting news to break into programming.
It does not. I go outside to wait and weed.
A patch of sky west of the sun bleeds from white
to cornflower. For an hour, morning

is a 40 watt bulb. Birds hop slower, but keep
peeping. The air chills, then warms.
The rooster crows, "Only this? Only this?"
I was ready to glimpse hidden stars,

to know light and darkness clearly defined.
I was prepared today to be startled.
I rise from something less than expected
but am not killed for being surprised.

Loose Woman

I am a loose woman.
When I am pregnant,
my joints roll like scales–
silken stones hard kissing
the shore of Lake Michigan.
When I am unmarried,
I am impossible
to keep straight, aligned–
serpentine, a river
caressing the Great Plains.
When I am raped,
I close my lids
to watch her slip
like shit into the
Grand Canyon nobody
visits. I slither up.

Moved by Emptiness

You've got an empty feeling, want to move
again. I want to stay. I like this house,
this quiet street, these friends. I know that you've
a tender spirit one blown word could dowse.
Your light burns dimly. Just your anger flares.
My family's close. The garden's good. But you
are husband—more than these. The God who cares
for me creates this welcome test. In lieu
of asking for my happiness, I choose
to pray for good from my distress, to turn
desire from what I love to what I lose
beside the road to righteousness. Why yearn
for my life but doubt it will be given?
Life is my carrot leading to heaven.

Mrs. Jacob Buller's Grave

I pull grass from your sunken stone grave face—
reaching without thinking, like a mother

who will push a stray hair from a daughter's eyes—
then apologize to a woman without a name

who may wish to erase her alias,
who may wish to express her vigor in the grass.

Mrs. Jacob Buller's Wedding

You held us close as Mother held me over the sea.
No one noticed my illness; we were not sent back.
We built with adobe on this prairie of my childhood
and womanhood. Cottonwoods call me
through tall grass to the creek to catch sunfish.
When the wild plums bear, I find them.
I would like to live at home. Yet, his wife
has been dead now six months. Women like me
are expected to be willing to help.

Standing still with Jacob for the photographer
under the tent, I watch his daughters, nearly my age,
laughing at their younger brothers' mimicry.
I left something at home—help me remember—
or it fell off the wagon as we moved my things
through the ruts linking our yard to his pasture—
something so ordinary, it may not have a name.

Old Story

There was the time
we sold most
of our wedding presents,

his souvenirs
from childhood vacations,
his Lincoln penny

collection, even
the 1909 SVBD,
the blue dress I wore

to my aunt's wedding
when I was six,
the wooden sewing rocker

with the back carved
in large resinous flowers,
and as much

as we had
that we could easily
leave behind.

We put the money
in our pockets
and made plans

for a trip
across the Southwest.
He welded two bikes

together and built
a platform between them
for our baby

and a platform in back
for our trunk.
He made

a canvas covering
for it all,
and it looked

like a buggy.
He would preach salvation.
I would wash diapers

by the campfire.
Our folks got scared.
Maybe we did, too.

Then a friend offered
a different way—
a little church

in the hills
that was living
on visions and songs.

We stayed there until
we were ready to start
for home again.

Well, it's a story
of youth, but
the grip of it holds

me still, that
we got as far
as we did, and

that we have
traveled lighter
since.

On Entering Grandma's House

The wallpaper becomes
our common skin,
rose following
tumbling rose,
pattern never ending
before beginning again.

Outside

Gospel of Mary

I leave the house at dusk to gather
whatever I need from the world for sleep.

Leaves in stairwells, muddy wrappers,
stars, bats, street and yard lights tie my dark

comforter's knots. It is a tradition; maybe
it is genetic—some stay inside, some must

leave to recognize themselves. The inside
of a house can equal the mass of the rest

of the universe. Black holes shed light.
If we do not live within, we must live

without. I walk the dark streets.
Great-grandma fished the creek

forever and eluded her daughter's family
and neighbors under those sandhill plums.

My dreams about working too hard
play out in her abandoned rooms.
I can take what I need from the darkness.
It gives out, dissolves, at the rate of stars,

trees, or plastic bags on barbed wire fences.

Photographs

I.
A waterfall or a constant wind
I could take, but this
highway outside my bedroom window
is loosening my bolts.

I drive slowly past For Sale signs.
He picks me up at work one day
and says, "Okay."
We get the kids
and drive into the country.

II.
Dad promised Mom
before I was born
a train ticket once a year
to Kansas.
We always took it.

In my memory, the prickly pear
blooms perfectly
in the sheltered place
of the back pasture
the whole time I am gone.

The pasture is as good
as an old photograph
I hold before me
looking for where
my smile comes from
and the tightness in my chest.

I will settle
when we get there.
Home is a place,
I'm telling you.
I feel as territorial
as a cat.

III.
Stars are apples,
the darkness a well-pruned dome
of laden branches.
From a certain point
on the Goessel road,
I see every yard light
in the Hillsboro-Lehigh valley—
fallen stars,
windfall apples.

Prodigal

I have photographs. I could show you
how happy we were. How much we wanted
to love him, taut foolish doormat puppies waiting
on the verge of abandonment to unthinking joy
in the recovery of the desperately gone.

But forgiveness is not a naïve gesture.
Think of a man forced to leave his home, wife, kids—
restraining orders, all that, forgiveness worn out.
But he left a dog chained to a backyard tree.
He left his hungry heart chained to a tree.

Time is not forgiveness. It was our fault it was starving—
we who were left too confused to feed a dog. Now
the chain remains buried in the crotch. Nothing grows
in the radius of the leash. Foul, hardened ground
rests in rain and drought, encroachment of weeds.

I took these photographs the morning I thought
the dog had forgiven me for leaving him at the pound
where I'd hoped others would save him. He'd gathered
strength, I thought, run fifty miles in the right direction.
When he appeared, I'd fallen into hugging, feeding,

brushing him. But he was only a farm dog on holiday,
claimed and hauled off by nightfall. Being uncertain
of the nature of my loss, I've tried to hold strays.
Forgiveness would seek positive identification.
I am returning from a great way off.

Psalm 1

She had been a holey-bucket,
fences-down, cows-out,
starling-shook,
milk-spilled,
dam-broken,
scared covey.

She had been
kin to prairie,
to wind.

Her feet were maps,
wandered by rivers.

Now she sprouts
hair roots and stares
at the trees.

Rearranging Furniture

for Jon

On my fiftieth birthday,
my old father says, "What do you think
of my crooked couch?" He means "angled."
It looks pretty good.

His rooms are always
clicking-kaleidoscope new.
His couch is thirty-two. He's bored, he says,
by his ordinary chores,

his vacuuming and such, and always
works to make them new.
Every couple weeks, when I was his
child, the couch moved to

a different spot. We moved on
an average of once
a year until I left home, and even
then, in our own moves, we each

held up our averages, nearly—I've lived
in forty-two places by now and had
eight couches since, two new. No new
houses—three so old, they were razed

by their next owners. My son
named for my father already owns
his first new couch;
he complains

his birthplace is gone.
I picture the old
wallpapered room, the antique bed,
the laundry brought in from the line

and piled on the dresser. I keep and lose
everything in abiding places. Every
arrangement is joy, every
shape of the breathtaking dust.

Red-Tailed Hawks
for Ryun

She's driving sixty-five south on K-15, late to church.
The road knows itself. She drives it blind, absorbed
in details that change with light, with the tilt of the earth,

hits the brakes—fifty-some migrating red-tailed hawks
stand staring into the south wind, fifty spaced in forty
stubble acres enclosed two sides by road, two by hedge.

Her son smashes his fist into the visor, *let's go, let's go.*

To keep their balance, they must self-center in the wind.

Remember

If I remember
everything
as myself,
the little spot I pick
which never heals
takes a number,
sits down,
looks around,
waits.

I believe what I think
is God lives inside
my head, sprouts tentacles
to connect with other heads
and forms a web
of high-mindedness

I often do not think
I possess, but I must,
even when
I do not
remember.

Riddles from Mary

Rock your children to riddle songs.
What once seemed right may now seem wrong.
Children leave home to find their own.
Shelter yourself in riddle songs.

I lost my home when I was young.
I have found my honor in having none.
In his father's house, I lost my son.
I have found my family by losing one.

An angel's riddles brought me hope.
I sang and danced with my womenfolk.
The prophet saw a sword in my soul.
Why does piercing make me whole?

I stretched and stretched for a child to grow.
Stretch to purpose. Let it go.
I am stretched again—does anyone know
the mother of God needs redemption? So,

I live with riddles to pass along
to my hundred times children and siblings, none
of whom have lived through birth only once.
We name each other blessed one.

Round House

In a round house balanced on a rocky cliff between ocean and mountain, its walls all windows opening onto the panoramic view, two women circle each other in a face-off with cameras raised, shutter fingers poised, focuses set. One shoots when she sees the other framed by the ocean. At that moment, the other's composure falls. Neither woman can see but both can now hear their hosts whispering accusations about the women's children. The one who framed her subject against the sea stays to face her invisible hosts, plots to live long in the house. The other who framed her opponent against the mountain flees; her figure recedes down the narrow, rocky beach.

Scissors

The only scissors I can keep
is the pair that is lost—my neighbor's.
How it came, I don't remember
if I ever knew. I imagine the children
got it mixed in their things at school.
But they say they didn't tell me that.

Or did I buy it at the grocery store
after the divorce? I was losing things
at the time and wanted something
no one would know about.

When you use a scissors on paper or plastic,
it dulls for use on cloth. You have to hide it
to keep it sharp. But even I have
taken the hidden one for paper.
So, maybe I brought it out, and then forgot

it was mine. It had that look of quality—
my neighbor has good things. It's mine
now. Lost is lost, a final home
from which you can't be severed.

Shingles, Socks, and Photographs

The sky that day must have been drunk,
its air unnatural, its conscience blocked.
It stalked us like a hunting cat.
Like a screaming cat, it pounced on the yard,
sinking its teeth into veins, shredding the house
and barn and car, flinging ravaged pieces far,
tearing branches of fruit and elm, twisting trunks
forever down, leaving remains of ragged tin,
nails, glass, shingles, socks and photographs.

This fall branches are out of proportion,
as are tall weeds on the bare foundation.
A mist lies where the house had been,
and the mist is an empty blanket
on the knees of a midwife moon.
The aching of mist brings no children,
but the aching of children for home
brings mist like a ghost in labor
breathing silent, ineffectual groans.

Silence

As the silence rises,
do your strings not tremble?
As the silence falls,
do your ears not ring?

The earth is netted with bones,
traced with trenches of death—
graves of heeled-in, cut-in,
planted-whole humans.

And dust-to-dust adobe churches
cover sacred bones—
delicate ribs and wrists,
small skulls—some broken, some whole.

Do your strings not tremble?
Do your ears not ring?

Storage Issues

*For, in the past, nothing is irrecoverably lost
    but everything irrevocably stored.* —Viktor E. Frankl

The cemetery she walks at dusk holds heat like her ancestors'
upstairs bedrooms in August. Her grandparents, their parents
and step-parents, brothers and sisters, half-brothers and half-
sisters, daughter, grandchild, and others of the congregation

lie labeled in orderly rows. For whom and what are these
kept? She sorted and cleaned upstairs before the auction:
boxes of gloves missing fingers, shoes with unrepaired soles,
unpatched overalls, wedding dresses, dolls with wardrobes,

hymn books, *True Stories*, grain receipts, feather pillows,
woolen comforters: everything sold or scattered then
into deeper storage. Where is that book now that should save
her soul? Where is that fabric that should protect her? Under

the moon's fine fingernail clipping, she wonders
what she may need and has not kept.

String Bag

Tying you in a string bag,
I carry you, fleshy excretion
of the wind, baby

that I may have to drop,
leave to die, may be able
to feed, make a cave for

until you walk away,
leave me barren
again in dead leaves.

Listen—crickets, frogs,
highway noises; I could
be anywhere before dawn.

Sunday Evening

The whole room ticks with the clock. Clean
lace slips from shelves like snow. Alone
with the snoring old man, she hears

other children returning to
the women in the kitchen and
the men on the porch. She'd fallen

asleep reading alone in the parlor.
Dusk holds her wrists and sits on her
knees. Light from the kitchen drifts down

the hall. She knows he will wake if
she moves to get up. No one will
remember to help her get out.

The Matchbox

I.
A woman's laughter,
a woman's milk,
some things a woman needs
to give, not keep.

We give our days to the farm.
Heinrich and I make it go.
We put our barrenness
out of our minds.

But now I have conceived—
after fifteen years!
Fullness of earth—to me!
Swelling my womb—my own!

The January sun
rises on my daughter's birth,
but sets on her fresh grave.
What I give back
I shall never recover.

II.
Papa took well
to the girls I brought home—
Emma, too old to adopt,
but Frieda, ours now,
and only one year younger
than Helena would have been.

When poor Mr. Franz
came to me in church
yesterday, begging me
to take his motherless
baby boy Ernest,
I knew, but I had to think.
I have been thinking all night—

harvest is over, my garden
almost done, Frieda
starts school in two weeks.
I could. I just need
to change out of my chore clothes
and hitch the buggy.

Papa does not always ask me
about everything; I, too,
can do as I like.
I must fix
a very good supper tonight.

III.
The empty matchbox
looks like an empty cradle.

Since Frieda died,
I will always have emptiness.

This fall I hear the children
pass our farm to school.

They belong to others,
but have some claim on me.

I fill matchboxes with candy,
a trinket, a new hankie,

peppernuts, and when I have enough,
wrap them for the Christmas program.

I will walk the mile
and a half under the stars.

The Old Land

You might be walking with your husband
in young wheat on a Sunday afternoon,
look down and pick up a hinge
or a small, thick edge of crockery.

You might explore the woods with your collie
and stumble upon three perfectly square stones.

You might hike along the hedgerow at dusk,
notice a tree slightly apart, come close,
and find two gravestones in the weeds.

You might picture a tepee
every time you drive past the east hayfield.

You might imagine eternity
in local terms.

The Revenger's Tragedy

Vindice
opens the play
holding the skull

of his fiancée.
Revenge feeds
on spirit as on flesh

the just worm.
Just one rock
through your window

would complete a cry
that breaks in my throat,
rips through my eyes.

One rock would end
this secret vigil,
this lying in wait

of reversal, this distance.
Never mind
you hoard

weapons as well.
I need to see
my face in a window

the wind cuts through.

Thy Waves

Deep calleth unto deep…all thy waves
*   and thy billows are gone over me.* —Psalm 42:7 (KJV)

What you can't control by being
cheerful, witty, optimistic, righteous or devout

bursts upon you
like a wall of water.

You can't hold on to anything
you thought was there—

it's gone,
and so are you.

Bobbing downstream,
later when you wake,

you find yourself a weakened
woman, the landscape changed,

no way to swim upstream,
no landmarks anyway.

Start over now, the way
fresh cut ravines must start again.

A seed blows in. How long
until the branching tree?

To My Daughter Jailed in Chicago:
03/20/2003

Now I feel how this world will end,
will be lost by saviors with power in the night.
On the street, in the cell, you who would not
move were hit by confusion, cuffs, abuse.
How fortunate you who were present.

How fortunate the couple who walked out
of the restaurant to find themselves in
the cordoned crowd, corralled by chance.

Who will tell me, who lives in the eye
of the swirling country, stays home
to plant, goes out to shop, dreams I sit
by your bed where you lie very still
as great shouldered men confer
in the shadows, I am fortunate?

Try This

Make it a duck,
full feathered and afloat,
with voice alone to steal your ease,
quiet and call to catch your throat.

Make it dive
out of sight or stretch wings
to be gone beyond trees
or land on grass.

Tame or wild, walk slowly
with duck food in your hand.
Do not make it a trinket,
a duck with eyes of glass.

Vachel Lindsay's Piano Moon

I am known here.
Intimately and at a distance, I am known.

The wind and I claim this.
No mountains here to speak of,

no ocean to reflect upon,
no rivers to lure.

I am myself here all a moon should be—
reflective, self-effacing, orbital,

lovely, comical, reliable,
mysterious, orderly, available.

All you have to do is look up and out.
Gaze upon the obvious orb. I have been

God, a breast, a face,
midwife, bucket, candle,

corn. I am everything you need.
Since I am all, you have to play.

Vision

I watch the woman walk the decline
toward the edge of the water.
She unfolds a fisher chair
upon the weedy bank, sits,
leans to look upon the water.

She is a reflection of an original

so that I know what I see
has depth beyond its reality
and know reality
because it is reflected.

She bruises the water, requiring
its return to perfection.

She needs more than one view

so that she will see light linked to branches,
so that she may confirm her imagination of sky,
so that she might see the depth of the surface.

We Place These Stones

The earth has heaved up rocks.
It can never put them back.
No one can,
not even Superman,
who did in a movie once,
but only by turning back time.

If I work a rock from the soil,
then decide to give it back,
something is changed,
if only a grain of earth
fallen into the hole, or a grub,
afterwards insecure.

We take these rocks, themselves
formed in a time of change,
as memorials to the upheaval
of death. We place these stones
on the heads of graves to remember
we cannot go back.

As to going forward,
the story divides. The way
I have been taught
veers off beside a vacated tomb,
a hard rock shoved aside.
On down that road we talk,

not about going back—
who can?—but of a man
who walked out living. If
we could get our hands
on him, what would he make
of grief and rubble?

We Wait for Words

between the parking lot and cemetery.
Lawn chairs and rows of blankets, damp with dew,
hold hushed, heavy-coated hopefuls waiting.

Although the sun is up, we wait
for the words "He indeed is risen,"
meaning Christ, who like so many others

also was taken. We wait in the sight
of the orderly graves. Will the bright,
newborn humans, full-grown, spring with dance

from moist, dark earth today? I turn to a woman
and ask, "What does the word on the gate mean—
Friedhof?" "That means place of peace."

Joy springs from our mouths. If these sleep,
do they dream with us and earth and heaven?

Wedding Rings

Some shine like the first weeks of conception,
a gleam or dread whose maturity with wonder
the mind and with alien intimacy the body fills;

some roll into a storm drain and grief sucks
only as in early miscarriage, too early to know
why the body screams, too early to bury;

some wear the groove in the finger that opposite
fingers fondle or fiddle with unconscious years
later, wheel ruts ending in an abandoned quarry;

and some never come like children never formed.
Who needs this much gold transformed,
she thinks, from unending leaden desire?

Wheat

A large spatula
skims down the sides of my soul
to the bottom,
then lifts up chocolate
cake batter emotions
when I see wind
moving tall wheat
in ripples and great long waves.

Wind touches wheat
like a farm girl
strokes a cat
on a summer morning
when the air is still early,
but the sun on its fur
is already hot—
it purrs a wave of tingling
and draws up for another sliding
of her whole hand
across its shining back.

Hear it rustling when it's ripe,
heads clacking together
like a whole village
playing gourd shakers
to a slow, serious folk song,
or a dirge.
From noon to the changing
of the yellow-white sun,
the festival goes on.
Then it cools to the moon
in a spent, dreamless peace.
Tomorrow's sun
will stir up
the troubles
that make them sing.

Winter Light

Rejection waits for winter's frozen blood
to run from coyote's body on the fence,
to rise with dirt, a fog red shade of mud.
Brown-silver light seeps droplets onto dense
ice, molten, brazen maize fields rich in gold
as Notre Dame's New Year's helmets trailing sun.
I gather remnants from this winter's cold
for weaving songs for me when I am done
with words he wishes said. I'll call the cops
if he sneaks back. His game is out of sea-
son; so is mine. This year our story tops
the local charts. To walk it out's the key.
I see brown trees hold white in milky light.
On blue days, brown bark's yellow. I'm all right.

Witness

No losses have not been seen
by some eyes. Nothing hides.
Maybe a caterpillar or flea
sees. Certainly cats see. This one

alone with me buries something
in his memory. We buried the old
white tomcat today. A tire track
rose over the curb, through the grass,
and across his stiff body. His voice
was that of an old smoker. I met

an uncle once who remembered
me as a baby. How I cried. We
don't see ourselves spinning; we
see the moon roll over our eyes.

Women's Work

I dig them up with care from softest humus.
Carrots travel darkness undisturbed.
They have to read their dreams to learn to do this.
I meditate on servings spiced and herbed.
Or yogurt is another way to work.
Warm milk to activate bacteria,
then insulate and never let a jerk
disturb its setting up. Wisteria
grows well here. Daisy. Lamb's ear. Mulberry.
I do not measure up or pull my weight.
Night fairies rise in moldy rings and bury
rejected strings of blood, and then they wait.
I will not measure up or pull my weight.
My knotted strings of blood rejected wait.

Yggdrasill

As whales in oceans and OEDs
in libraries are grand
yet feed on tiny things like plankton
and origins of sound,
so trees in earth are grand and feed
on gasses, dissolved minerals,
and strengths and durations
of sunlight. Trees grow slowly into
and around as well as support,
weird, fantastic details, like old cities,
perhaps also like ourselves who,
like visible fractions of the ash's
gnarled roots and shadowed branches,
show timeless invisible accretions
of overarching form.

Credits

"Breaking Bud," *The Mennonite*, May 23, 1995.

"Come Close," *The Christian Leader*, December 1993; *Voice*, January-February 1995.

"Dreamers," *Christian Living*, January-February 1992.

"Four Sticks," *Festival Quarterly*, Fall 1991. "Four Sticks" and "The Old Land" were first published in *Festival Quarterly*, Fall 1991, page 17. They are used here with permission of Good Books (www.GoodBooks.com). All rights reserved.

"Girls Playing Church," *Mikrokosmos*, Spring 2003.

"Grandma," *Lines*, 1991; *Voice*, May 1994.

"How Can We Know?" *The Gallery*, 2007.

"How Much More," *The Mennonite*, May 2, 2000.

"In the City at Twenty," *The Mennonite*, May 24, 1994.

"It Was the Kind," *Porcupine*, Winter 2006.

"Knowledge of Birds," *Women of the Plains: Kansas Poetry* (anthology), 1995.

"Leaves on the River," *The Mennonite*, October 4, 2005.

"Leaving Wichita Late," *Mikrokosmos*, Spring 2003.

"Living under Authority," *First Things: A Monthly Journal of Religion and Public Life*, October 1995.

"Old Story," *Window to Mission*, October-November 1989.

"On Entering Grandma's House," *Lines*, 1991; *Voice*, May 1994.

"Prelude," *Mennonite Life*, September 1992 ("Photographs").

"Prodigal," *The Penwood Review*, Spring 2007.

"Riddles from Mary," *Window to Mission*, Winter 1996.

"Shingles, Socks and Photographs," *The Mennonite*, October 11, 1994.

"Silence," *Voice*, April 1995.

"The Matchbox," *The Mennonite*, December 22, 1992.

"The Old Land," *Festival Quarterly*, Fall 1991.

"Thy Waves," *Women of the Plains: Kansas Poetry* (anthology), 1995.

"To My Daughter Jailed in Chicago: 3/20/03," *The Mennonite*, November 4, 2003.

"Try This," *Lines*, 1991.

"Vision," *Mikrokosmos*, Spring 2001.

"We Place These Stones," *Voice*, May 1991.

"We Wait for Words," *Mennonite Life*, September 1992.

"Wheat," *The Mennonite*, June 14, 1988.

"Yggdrasill," *The Gallery*, 2007.

The Author

Suzanne Kay Miller, born in northern Indiana in 1956, has also lived in Florida, Ohio, Oregon, Illinois, and Kansas. She studied at Kansas City School of Watchmaking, Hesston College (A.A. in Liberal Arts), Tabor College, Bethel College, and Wichita State University (B.A. in English; M.F.A. in Creative Writing).

During the years she wrote these poems, she raised her four children, worked a variety of part-time jobs, and earned degrees. Currently, she teaches writing at Friends University and is at work on another book of poems. She lives with her husband, Jim, in Wichita, Kansas.

www.ingramcontent.com/pod-product-compliance
Lightning Source LLC
Chambersburg PA
CBHW030002050426
42451CB00006B/92